PEGASUS ENCYCLOPEDIA LIBRARY

World History
MIDDLE AGES

Edited by: Tapasi De and Pallabi B. Tomar
Managing editor: Tapasi De
Designed by: Vijesh Chahal, Anil Kumar and Rohit Kumar
Illustrated by: Suman S. Roy, Tanoy Choudhury
Colouring done by: Vinay Kumar, Sonu, Kiran Kumari & Pradeep Kumar

CONTENTS

Introduction 3
The Byzantiums 5
A new identity 6
The Franks 8
Charlemagne, the memorable ruler 9
Rise of Islam 10
Middle ages in America 12
Khmer Empire 17
The Vikings 19
Europe in the Middle Ages 21
Medieval castles and cathedrals 22
Medieval theatre 24
Black Death 25
Crusades 26
The Mongols 27
Remarkable people of the Middle Ages 29
Test Your Memory 31
Index 32

Introduction

The Middle Ages was a period of about a thousand years that lasted from the fall of the Roman Empire to the beginning of the Renaissance. Interestingly, the people of the Renaissance period named this era 'Middle Ages' as it lay between the ancient and the modern times.

Petrarch, the notable writer and philosopher who lived in the early 1300s described this period as the **Dark Ages** because it seemed to be a period of decline of human achievement, especially when compared to the vast cultural accomplishments of the Ancient Greeks and Romans.

Of course, the period of the Middle Ages was not without its great works of art and literature. The works of art created in the Middle Ages were almost exclusively based on religion and the teachings of the Church. It was during the Middle Ages that Christianity spread among the migrating groups of people who began to settle in Europe.

Historians usually divide this era into three smaller periods— the **Early Middle Ages**, the **High Middle Ages**, and the **Late Middle Ages**.

The **Early Middle** Ages began with the downfall of the Roman Empire. Germanic people invaded the Roman Empire, the Visigoths settled in Spain, the Vandals in North Africa, Ostrogoths in Italy and the Franks in France. The Huns formed a European empire which collapsed after a while. The Angles and the Saxons invaded England. The Vikings invaded northern France and raided the Mediterranean. Again, the Lombards replaced the Ostrogoths in Italy and the Slavs invaded Eastern Europe.

The **High Middle** Ages started about 1000 AD, when the modern countries of Europe began to take form. After the Norman Conquest in 1066, the beginnings of England, France and Germany took place. Throughout the High Middle Ages, most of the people of Europe were fighting against the Islamic Empire to take back the Eastern Mediterranean region, especially Jerusalem for Christianity. These holy wars were called the **Crusades**.

Crusades

MIDDLE AGES

In the **Late Middle Ages**, the Mongol Empire controlled most of Asia, and encouraged trade along the **Silk Road**. By the early 1300s, however, Europe was under the spell of war and disease. England and France began to fight the **Hundred Years War**, which made both England and France much poorer. These wars were made much worse by the **Black Death**, an epidemic which spread to Europe killing millions of people.

After the plague, Europe looked very different. The wars were over. The end of the Silk Road forced traders to look for other ways to get things from China and India. Explorers began to try find a way to sail from Europe around Africa to China.

It was in the late Middle Ages that European scholars became more interested in studying the world around them. They began to explore new lands. The new age in Europe was eventually called the **Renaissance** which ended the dark middle ages. Renaissance is a French word that means 'rebirth'. Historians consider the Renaissance to be the beginning of modern age.

Black Death

4

The Byzantiums

In A.D. 395 Rome was split into two separate empires, in order to make it easier to rule. The western empire was called **Rome**, while the eastern empire took the name of **Byzantium** with its capital at **Constantinople**. By A.D. 500 Rome began to decline and was soon conquered. The safety, privileges and the stability enjoyed by the Romans were suddenly replaced by a constant danger and uncertainty. The Byzantine Empire on the other hand lasted for another 1,000 years!

It cannot be said that the Byzantine Empire was centre of peace in the perilous middle ages. On the contrary, its long history was full of numerous wars and remarkable internal struggle. Nevertheless, Byzantium remained the most stable nation of the middle ages. Its central location between Western Europe and Asia not only enriched its economy and its culture but allowed it to serve as a barrier against aggressive barbarians from both areas. Its rich tradition (strongly influenced by the church) preserved ancient knowledge on which art, architecture, literature and technological achievements were built.

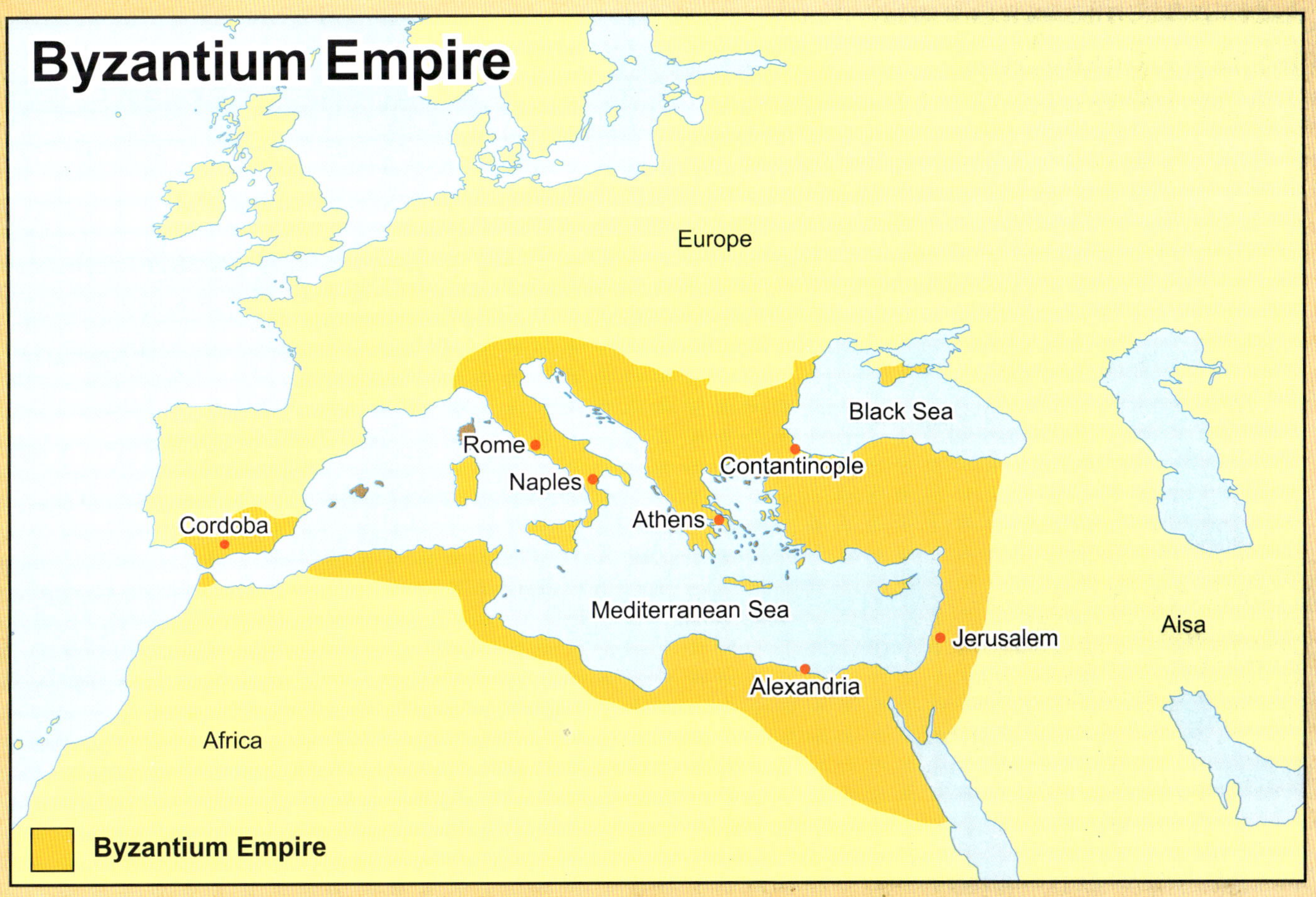

Byzantium Empire

A new identity

A new identity

While it is true that Byzantium was created by splitting the Roman Empire, they quickly moved away from the Roman traditions forming a new and distinct culture of their own. The Byzantiums were considerably proud of their nation and did not consider themselves Romans!

With time, the official language of the Byzantines became Greek, rather than the Latin which was used by the Romans. The Byzantines were Christians, but they did not follow the Catholic faith of the Romans. Instead, they developed their own version of Christianity.

Constantinople

The capital city of Constantinople located on a peninsula, has a natural geographic protection from invasion from all three sides and its fourth side was fortified with a network of three walls that withstood direct attack. The city was named after the Roman Emperor Constantine who had established this city realizing its strategic position.

The economy of Constantinople was stable. Abundant food supply and advanced civil engineering provided a high standard of living. Literacy was more widespread there than in any other nation in the Middle Ages. Intellectual and artistic endeavours thrived too. The city of Constantinople quickly grew, becoming the wealthiest city in the Roman Empire, even wealthier than the city of Rome itself!

A new identity

Emperor Justinian

When the Byzantine Empire was at its peak, a powerful Emperor called Justinian came to the throne at the age of 44. Justinian was a wise ruler who wanted his people to be successful and comfortable. He initiated a number of reforms to help make the lives of his subjects better. One of these important reforms was regarding the rights of women. Justinian granted women the right to buy land and own property. Emperor Justinian encouraged music, art and drama. He build new roads, bridges, aqueducts, baths and a variety of other public works. He built a cathedral in the heart of Constantinople which he named Hagia Sophia which stands even till today.

The Byzantine Art

The Byzantine Art movement which began around A.D. 330 in the Eastern Roman Empire included architecture, painting and all other forms of visual arts. Centered in the capital city of Constantinople, (Istanbul today) of the Byzantium Empire, Byzantine Art was centralized in the Orthodox Church. The churches were decorated with richly coloured paintings. Most of the buildings, walls, domes, vaults and floors were covered by mosaic tiles illustrating both colourful and charming images of Christ, Virgin Mary, the saints and the apostles often in the company of a Bishop and cherubs.

Hagia Sophia

The Hagia Sophia is a domed basilica. It has four minarets at its corners that were added at different times. It stands atop the first hill of Constantinople surrounded by the waters of the Sea of Marmara, the Bosphorus and the Golden Horn on three sides. It was built by Justinian I between 532 and 537. When the Ottoman conquered Constantinople in 1453, Islamic worship began in this holy structure. Now it is a museum.

The Franks

The Franks were one of the several West Germanic tribes who entered the late Roman Empire and established a kingdom in an area that covers part of modern France and Germany.

The Franks divided their kingdom into many partitions and repartitions as they divided their property among their surviving sons. Due to this practice, there is difficulty in describing precisely the dates and physical boundaries of any of the Frankish kingdoms and to know about the specific rulers of each territory.

The earliest Frankish history is quite unclear. Modern scholars have suggested that the Frankish people emerged from the unification of various earlier, smaller Germanic groups inhabiting the Rhine valley and lands immediately to the east.

The concept of the Franks as a community was first realized under the reign of the Merovingian dynasty. After AD 700, the Merovingians gradually lost control of the Frankish kingdom to the Carolingians, a family of ambitious landowners who served as court advisors to the Merovingians.

The most notable of all the Frankish rulers was **Charlemagne (Charles the Great)**.

> The Franks were tough warriors who went to the battles with shaven heads and topknots wearing armours. They were formidable cavalry fighters. The Franks defeated the Visigoths, Gauls, Romans who tried to come in their way of expansion.

The Palatine Chaple at Aachen, Germany (Carolingian architecture)

Charlemagne, the memorable ruler

Charlemagne was one of Europe's most successful monarchs. He was the king of the Franks who came to power after his father, Pepin the Short.

He was an able administrator of a vast territory, had a fair judicial system and also revived the arts. Charlemagne converted most of the people to Christianity and he was justly honored for his military and religious activities. On Christmas day of the year AD 800, Pope Leo III (795-816) crowned Charlemagne 'Charles Augustus, Emperor of the Romans,' and made him the first **Holy Roman Emperor**.

Astonishing fact

One of the most important things Charlemagne did for the world was to turn his castle into a learning centre by inviting scholars from all over the world. He used his scholars to create illuminated manuscripts (pages with gold cover) that preserved knowledge during the Dark Ages.

Charlemagne was over 6 ft. tall, had blonde hair and he was always happy. He never walked. He always strode. He knew everyone in his castle by their names!

Rise of Islam

Islam is a religion that inspires its followers to follow the path of honesty and humanity like all other religions. Prophet Mohammed is considered to be the founder of Islam and he played a vital role in spreading the teachings of Islam. Just as Quran is the last word revealed by God, Prophet Mohamed is the last messenger of God and the last Prophet.

Birth of Prophet Mohammed

Prophet Mohammed was born to a lady called Amina in 570 A.D. He was born in Mecca in Saudi Arabia. He belonged to the Quraish tribe. His father Abdullah passed away much before he was born and he lost his mother when he was six years old. Muhammad was looked after by his grandfather Hazrat Abdal Muttalib at that time. Later, his uncle brought him up as a successful and respected merchant.

When Prophet Mohammed grew up, he often used to meditate in the caves of Mt. Hira in a mountain called the Mountain of light. This cave was close to Mecca. It was the holy month of Ramzan when one day Mohammed heard a heavenly voice while meditating. It was the voice of Angel Gabriel. Mohammed was forty years old at that time.

When Angel Gabriel appeared for the first time she said to Muhammad, "Iqraa," meaning 'read or recite'. Muhammad replied, "I cannot read," as he did not know how to read or write. Angel Gabriel then embraced him until he reached the limit of his endurance and after releasing said, "Iqraa". Muhammad's answer was the same as before. Gabriel repeated the embrace and asked him to repeat a few lines on God's power and kindness.

Mecca

Mecca is a city in Saudi Arabia to which the Muslims turn to when they pray and millions of people travel there as pilgrimage. The pilgrims circle the Black stone which is believed by Muslims that it was given to Abraham by Angel Gabriel.

Rise of Islam

Muhammad was so puzzled and horror-struck by the whole experience of the **revelation** that he fled from the cave of Mt. Hira. When he reached his home, tired and frightened, he asked his wife to cover him with a blanket. When he gained his normal disposition, his wife Khadijah asked him about the reason of his great anxiety and fear.

After hearing the whole story she assured him by saying, "Allah will never let you down because you are kind to all, you speak only the truth, you help the poor, the orphan and the needy and you are an honest man." Khadijah then consulted her cousin Waraqa who was an old, saintly man possessing knowledge of scriptures. Waraqa confirmed to her that the visitor was none other than the Angel Gabriel who had come to Moses. He then added that Muhammad was the **Prophet.**

Khadijah accepted the revelation as truth and was the first person to accept Islam. Next, Muhammad's cousin Ali, his servant Zyad and his friend Abu Bakr followed Islam. She supported her husband in every hardship.

Prophet Mohammed had to face lots of resistance when he started preaching Islam. Some people regarded him as a fool and some even humiliated him to a great extent. He was opposed mostly by people who believed in idol worship. He had to also face oppositions from the people who worshiped multiple Gods. However, he was supported by some foreigners and some downtrodden people.

Though Mecca was Mohammed's native city, he was in danger there after the death of his wife Khadija and Uncle Abu Talib. Powerful tribes in Mecca wanted to kill Mohammed. At the same time many of his followers from Medina came for a pilgrimage and to meet him. The number of his followers in Medina was increasing day by day.

Mohammed accepted the invitation from twelve important clans from Medina to become the chief authority of their community. He was protected physically also by them. Prophet Mohammed played an important role in developing Medina as the first Islamic state. He led Medina not only religiously but also politically.

Mohammed's last sermon was known as 'Khutbatul Wada'. During this sermon he addressed a large number of people. The soul objective of his sermon was to encourage people to spread Islam. He explained a way of life that a Muslim should have during his last sermon.

Prophet Mohammed died after ten years of his relocation to Medina in 632 A.D. Before his death, Muhammad performed two months of Hajj and he fell ill after his pilgrimage. He preached Islam until the last moment of his life. Prophet Mohammed dedicated his entire life for spreading the message of **Allah**. Through his preaching he was successful in making Islam an immortal and unique religion throughout the world.

Middle ages in America

Many unique civilizations grew in the north, central and south America in the Middle Ages. The three best known civilizations among all of them were the **Maya**, **Aztec** and **Inca** which were contemporaneous with Medieval Europe. While the chronology of the Maya, Aztec, and Inca are fairly well developed, the dating of the early civilizations and the early history of human settlement in the Americas is subject to controversy.

Mayan Civilization

Mayan civilization is one of the greatest civilizations in the world. It is a Mesoamerican civilization noted for the only known fully developed written language of the pre-Columbian Americas. Mesoamerica is a geographical region that extends throughout Central America and Mexico. It is worth noting that the Mayas developed the most accurate calendars known. They also mastered astrology and

Mayan ruins

Middle ages in America

Mayan Calendar

The Mayas were extremely good at calculating time. They developed over 17 calendars, each with a different purpose. In the modern era, we marvel at the precision and complexity of these calendars, without understanding how they were actually used. The solar calendar (Haab) calculated the year more accurately than our present one, but was based on 360 days.

Mayan-speaking people filled an area of the modern Yucatan peninsula, Guatemala, Belize and parts of the Mexican states Chiapas and Tabasco, Honduras and El Salvador. Throughout this large part of Mesoamerica are thousands of ancient Mayan ruins with temples and palaces, carved monuments and hieroglyphic texts. About six million present day descendants of the ancient Mayans still live in this area, speaking over 30 Maya dialects.

Mayan ceramic

mathematics and produced exquisite art on ceramics and murals. The engineering accomplishments of the Mayas spread over 100 centuries. It was unrivalled by even modern civilizations until the 19th century.

Mayan mural

Aztecs

The Aztecs or more accurately, the Mexicas, were Mesoamerican people of central Mexico in the 14th, 15th and 16th centuries. They were a civilization with a rich mythology and cultural heritage. Their capital was Tenochtitlan built on raised islets in Lake Texcoco which lies in modern-day Mexico City.

The Aztecs founded a strong secure central government. This helped provide stability and allowed the empire to thrive for a long time. At the top of this government was the royal family, headed by an emperor or a king. The emperor maintained his control over the empire through the use of his large and powerful army.

The main contribution of the Aztec rule was the development of a system of communications between the conquered cities. In Mesoamerica, they had no animals for transport or wheeled vehicles. So the roads were designed for travelling on foot with rest houses and guards for the traveller's security.

The main deity in the Mexica religion was their **Sun God** and **War God**, **Huitzilopochtli**.

The Aztec people were lovers of art. Song and poetry were highly regarded in the Aztec society. Poetry was considered to be the only occupation worthy of an Aztec warrior in times of peace.

Slavery

The slavery that existed in the Aztec society was very different from what Europeans of the same period established in their colonies. First, slavery was not hereditary; that is, a slave's children were free. A slave could have possessions and even own other slaves. Slaves could buy their liberty and slaves could be set free on certain occasions.

Middle ages in America

The Inca Empire

When the gold-seeking Spanish people reached Peru in 1532, they encountered a vast empire of a Quechua-speaking people called the Incas. The great civilization of the Incas extended along the Pacific coast of South America from modern Ecuador southward to central Chile and inland across the Andes.

The Andes Mountains dominated the Incan society. The mountain peaks were worshipped as gods. The Inca believed in reincarnation. They believed that those who obeyed the Incan moral code—ama suwa, ama llulla, ama quella (do not steal, do not lie, do not be lazy) went to live in the sun's warmth while others spent their eternal days on the cold Earth.

The social structure of the Inca Empire varied from one place to another, but they did have some basic structure. On top was the **Sapa Inca** or the Emperor. Then came the **nobles** who were often the priests and relatives of the past Emperors or the current ones. After this, there were **craftsmen** and **architects**. Then came the **working class**—the farmers. At the bottom were the **slaves** and **peasants**.

When we talk of Inca art, we must remember that architecture was the most important. The main example of this is the capital city of Cusco. The breathtaking site of Machu Picchu was constructed by Inca engineers. The stone temples constructed by the Incas used a mortarless construction.

Sapa Inca

Machu Picchu

Machu Picchu

The ancient city of Machu Picchu was discovered in 1911 by an American historian Hiram Bingham. Some believe that it was a country estate; some believe it was a religious site and some believe that it was a city high in the Andes mountains. Explorers found ruins of temples, palaces, fortresses and a royal tomb. They found remains of the stone aqueducts that brought water into the city. They also found remains of terrace gardens and homes for farmers, nobles, and priests. Intihuatana or ceremonial pyramids were also found. It was built to speak to their Sun God, Inti.

Afterlife

Like the ancient Egyptians, the Incas believed in afterlife. They mummified their dead. The family held a funeral for eight days. Women in mourning wore black clothes for about a year. They also cut their hair really short.

The bodies and tombs of the dead were carefully tended to. The mummies of dead rulers remained in their palaces. These rulers were treated as if they were still alive. On special occasions, their mummies were carried through the streets.

The mighty empire of the Incas came to an end when in A.D. 1533 the Spanish arrived in South America. Hungry for territory and for converts to Christianity, the Spanish wiped out the Incan Empire completely. But to this day, many descendants of the Incans still live in the nations of Chile, Bolivia, Peru and Ecuador.

The Inca Empire 1463 - 1532

Khmer Empire

The **Khmer or Angkor Civilization** was an ancient kingdom of south-east Asia in the 6th century. It stretched as far as the modern Thailand-Burma Border in the West and Wat Phou of Laos in the North during its peak time. The capital was established in the area of Angkor by the king Yasovarman I.

The Angkor period, the golden age of Khmer civilization, saw the empire at its greatest extent. In this period many Indian scholars, artists and religious teachers visited the Khmer court and Sanskrit literature flourished with royal patronage. Historians believe that the Khmer civilization was largely formed by Indian cultural influences. The main religions that flourished were Buddhism and Hinduism at that time.

The Khmers were brilliant in the fields of architecture and sculpture. The earliest known Khmer monuments were isolated towers of brick. Small temples set on stepped pyramids appeared next. It was after this that the covered galleries began to be build. Brick was largely abandoned in favour of stone. Khmer architecture reached its height with the construction of Angkor Wat by King Suryavarman II and Angkor Thom by Jayavarman VII.

Yasodharapura

Yasodharapura was the first city to be built at the Angkor site. The city was built during the reign of King Yasovarman I after the palace in the previous capital at Roluos was burned during his struggle to come to power after the death of the previous king, his father. The later succeeding capitals built in the area were also called Yasodharapura. Yasodharapura in Sanskrit means 'Holy City'.

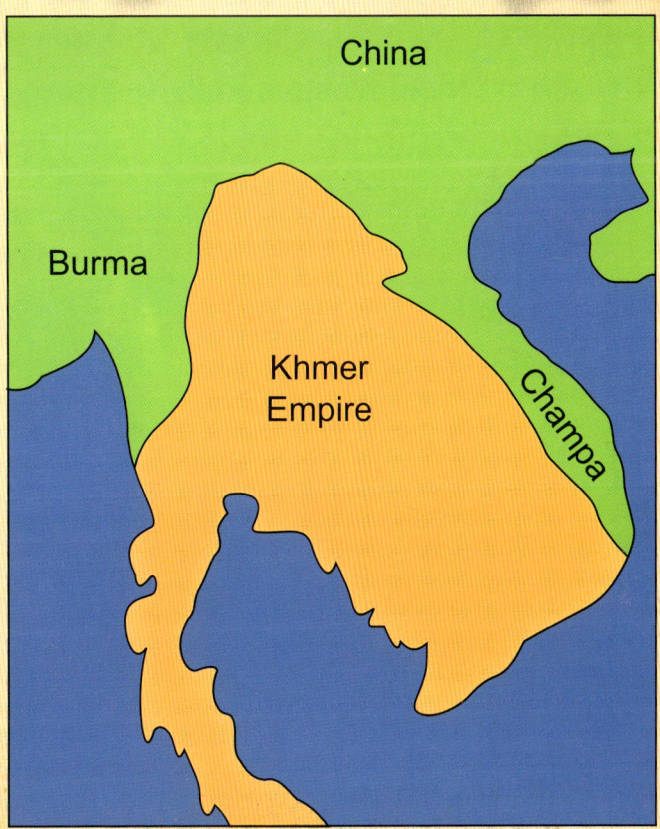

MIDDLE AGES

Life of the people

Most of the information about the life of the Khmer common people come from the Chinese Chronicle written by Zhou Daguan who was a Chinese ambassador of Yuan Dynasty. He visited the Angkor Empire in 1296 and travelled widely inside the kingdom for a year. As Zhou had resided with the local people in various circumstances, he gave fairly an accurate picture about the life and activities of the common men in the Khmer kingdom.

It is noteworthy that all trades in Khmer were carried out by women. In the market place, there were no shops, and the female vendors sold their goods and products on the mats which are spread on the ground. The Khmer people cooked their food in the earthen pots. The ladle sticks were made up from the coconut shells.

As the palaces and the houses in the Angkor Empire were mainly made up on unendurable materials such as woods and thatched leaves, they left no traces to the present day, except the various Khmer temples which were built with bricks and stones.

Angkor Vat

The structure of Angkor Vat was built as a temple which has immense significance in the life of the Cambodians even today. It serves as a national symbol for them in the present day. It was initially dedicated to Lord Vishnu but was later on was used for Buddhism. This unique structure is built primarily of sandstone. It is surrounded by a moat which makes reaching it through the jungles a bit difficult.

Angkor Vat

The Vikings

The Vikings were Indo-European people from Scandinavia (modern Denmark, Norway and Sweden), who began raiding into Europe and even into the Mediterranean Sea raiding Sicily and southern Italy during the middle ages. Most of them left their homes in search of wealth and adventure. They travelled in medium-sized sailing ships.

The Vikings were excellent warriors. They used their light weight ships to secretly attack their victims, and then retreat before their enemies could even fight back. They were brutal, and often killed their victims after torturing them.

Social life of the Vikings

Upper class Vikings were called Jarls. Below them were a class of farmers and craftsmen called Karls. At the bottom was a class of slaves called thralls. Slavery was common in the world at that time. It was accepted as an inevitable part of life.

While on their raids, the Vikings captured women and children and made them slaves. They were sold in markets and they had no rights. Slaves did the hardest and the most unpleasant work.

Viking merchants imported glass and silk from the Byzantine Empire. They also imported spices, fine wool and wine. They exported slaves, furs, beeswax, honey and walrus ivory.

Viking craftsmen included blacksmiths, bronze smiths, coopers, leather tanners, saddlers, shoemakers and other men who made leather goods like purses and belts. Some craftsmen carved bone and antler into goods like combs.

The Vikings also had their own form of writing. The Viking alphabet was called the **futhark** and the 16 individual letters were called **runes**. They were made of straight and diagonal lines, which were carved into wood or stone.

MIDDLE AGES

The Thing

The Viking law court was called the Thing. Every year local people came together for several days. Any freeman who had a problem could raise the matter there. His neighbours would listen and give the judgement. Any person who refused to obey the Thing's verdict, became an outlaw and were ordered to be killed at once!

Vikings and Christianity

For many centuries the Vikings worshiped a variety of gods and goddesses. However, as they expanded their territories and built colonies in distant lands, they came into close contact with the Western Europe. Most of Western Europe at that time were converted to Christianity. Eventually, most Vikings became converted to Christianity as well. This conversion helped to civilize them in many ways.

Europe in the Middle Ages

The Medieval period is the longest era in the European history and is considered to be very complex too. It is generally defined as the period of European history from the fall of Rome (5th century) to the Renaissance (15th century). During this era, the Church became the dominant influence. Life was more primitive when compared to the Roman times. There were barbarian elements also. Society was dominated by a single, militant religion. Medieval Christian Europe faced several major military threats too. The Huns, northern Germanic tribes, the Vikings frequently raided medieval Europe resulting in numerous battles.

Feudalism in Europe

After the fall of the Roman Empire, the Feudal system developed in Europe. Feudalism was an economic and social system based on the distribution of land in exchange for allegiance and service. The system was based on the king granting land to his important noblemen who became **barons**. These land grants became hereditary. The king also granted land to the Church. These nobles in exchange pledged loyalty to the king and to provide soldiers and supplies in times of war. The great nobles in turn divided their fiefdom among lesser **lords** or **knights** who became his vassals.

Most Europeans were peasant farmers working on the land of a Feudal nobleman—the lord of the manor. They did not own their land, but were allowed to work on it in exchange for amount of the crop and labour when required. As the Feudal system developed, the peasants or serfs became tied to the land and were not allowed to leave it without the permission of the lord of the manor. The Feudal system began to weaken in Western Europe by the 16th century, but persisted much longer in Eastern Europe.

William the Conqueror was an extremely powerful medieval king who kept under him one fourth of England's land and distributed the rest to his followers in return for loyalty and allegiance.

Medieval castles and cathedrals

Castles

The greatest architectural achievement of the medieval era were the castles that are found all over Europe. These castles were an integral part of the medieval era and the feudal system.

Windsor Castle

The largest castle in England, the Windsor Castle is one of the main residences of the queen and sprawls over 13 acres. The first castle on this site was set up by William the Conqueror in about 1070.

Windsor is the only royal castle that has been continuously occupied since the Middle Ages and is the largest inhabited castle in the world. The castle offers excellent views of the countryside. The early castle was almost built of wood. Windsor is still a principal royal residence and much of the castle is not open to the public.

Edinburgh Castle

Edinburgh Castle is a castle fortress located in Edinburgh, Scotland. As one of the most important fortresses in the Kingdom of Scotland, Edinburgh Castle has been involved in many historical conflicts from the Wars of Scottish Independence in the 14th century, up to the Jacobite Rising of 1745. From the later 17th century, the castle became a military base with a large garrison.

During the middle ages pilgrims made long journeys to visit holy places. In England, the most famous shrine was that of St. Thomas Becket at Canterbury.

Medieval castles and cathedrals

St. Peter's Basilica

St. Peter's Basilica

St. Peter's Basilica is a major basilica in the Vatican City, an enclave of Rome. St. Peter's remains one of the holiest sites in Christendom. Originally founded by Constantine in 324, St. Peter's Basilica was rebuilt in the 16th century by Renaissance masters including Bramante, Michelangelo and Bernini.

St. Peter's Basilica stands on the traditional site where Peter, the apostle who is considered the first pope, was crucified and buried.

Notre Dame Cathedral

Notre Dame Cathedral is a beautiful cathedral in Paris which is an important example of French Gothic architecture, sculpture and stained glass art. It is the most popular monument in all of France, beating even the Eiffel Tower with 13 million visitors each year!

Notre Dame Cathedral

Medieval theatre

The origin of the medieval drama was in religion. The Church forbade the theatre which had developed during the Romans as it was immoral and licentious. But once this immoral theatre had disappeared, the Church allowed and itself contributed to the gradual development of a new drama, which was not only moral but also pious.

The 15th century saw the beginning of the **Mystery Plays**. These plays were often devoted to a saint, and, in extraordinary cases, even represented matters which were not religious.

Miracle Plays, another kind of medieval religious play was based on non-scriptural legends of saints or of the Virgin Mary. The term is often confusingly applied also to the mystery plays, which form a distinct body of drama based on biblical stories.

Geoffrey Chaucer was an English author, poet, philosopher, bureaucrat, courtier and diplomat. Although he wrote many works, he is best remembered for his unfinished work The Canterbury Tales. He is sometimes called the father of English literature.

Astonishing fact

The chimneys that are used now were actually invented in the middle ages. This made it possible to make fireplaces.

Black Death

In October, 1347, a deadly disease entered Europe through a port in Sicily. The ships docked for a long time there became full of rats which were carrying infected fleas. As the rats died, the fleas had to find new carriers many of whom were humans. Within days, hundreds of people began dying each day from this illness. People fled to the countryside, only to spread the disease even further. By November that year, the island of Sicily had submitted completely, and by December, the plague had reached the mainland of Italy and much of Southern Europe. This frightful infection was called the **Black Death**.

By the next year, the plague engulfed all of Europe. By late 1351, it had completed its destruction of Europe. A third of the population had died in only four years!

MIDDLE AGES

Crusades

The Crusades were a series of holy wars during the medieval era which took place between the Muslims and the Christians. In 1076, the Muslims had captured Jerusalem— the most holy land of the Christians. Jesus had been born in nearby Bethlehem and Jesus had spent most of his life in Jerusalem. So, Jerusalem for a true Christian is considered to be the 'City of God'. However, Jerusalem was equally important for the Muslims too as Mohammed, the founder of Islam, had been there. After the Muslims had taken over Jerusalem, they prohibited the Christians from entering. This angered the Christians all over and from Rome Pope Urban II called upon the Christians to free Jerusalem from the Muslims. And so, a series of war took place which lasted nearly for 200 years. There were nine wars in all.

The effects of the Crusades

The effects of the Crusades on Europe during the Middle Ages were an important factor in the progress of civilization. The effects of the Crusades influenced the wealth and power of the Catholic Church, political matters, commerce, feudalism, intellectual development, social effects and material effects as well. One of the very positive effects of the Crusades is that they prompted the famous voyages of discovery of new lands.

Astonishing fact

One of the most unusual military expeditions ever was performed in 1191, during the third Crusade, when Richard the Lion-Hearted captured the city of Acre. The inhabitants were kept inside, when King Richard had his soldiers throw 100 beehives over the walls! The people in the fortress surrendered at once.

Saladin was the greatest of all the Muslim leaders who had taken over Jerusalem but in 1192 made peace with King Richard 1 and allowed the Christians to enter Jerusalem.

The Mongols

The Mongols were nomadic people who lived in central Asia in the area stretching from the Ural Mountains to the Gobi desert. They were extremely ferocious people who sent waves of fear and trauma throughout Asia and Europe. They were formidable cavalry warriors who overwhelmed their enemies easily. They preferred to keep their hands free to use the bow and arrow or throw lance at the enemy.

The Mongol Empire emerged from the integration of Mongol and Turkish tribes in the region of modern day Mongolia under the leadership of Genghis Khan (meaning 'lord of all'). Genghis Khan proclaimed himself the ruler of all Mongols in 1206. The empire grew rapidly under his leadership and then that of his successors who sent invasions in every direction. After the death of Genghis Khan, his grandson Kublai Khan succeeded him.

In 1276 AD, the Mongols invaded and took over China. Their empire stretched from India and Russia to northern China and Korea. In 1276 the Mongols captured the Sung capital at Hangzhou, and by the next few years they controlled the whole of China. Kublai Khan moved the capital of the Mongol Empire from Karakorum in Central Asia to Beijing, China. In 1271, when he was 56, Kublai Khan declared himself the Emperor of China.

Kublai Khan

Kublai Khan was the fourth son of Tulë and the grandson of Genghis Khan, the founder of the Mongol Empire. Strong, brave and intelligent, Kublai was Genghis's favourite grandson. He had accompanied his father, Tulë, in battles as a child. By the age of twelve he was a skilled horseman and his reputation as a warrior grew as he became older. Kublai was seventeen when his father died.

Administration

Under Kublai, the Mongols adopted a divide-and-rule policy. The Mongols and central Asians remained separate from Chinese life. The superior rule of the Mongols was assured by dividing the population of China into four social classes— the Mongols, the central Asians, the northern Chinese and Koreans and the southern Chinese. The first two classes enjoyed extensive privileges; the third class held an intermediate position; and the southern Chinese, the most numerous of all, were practically barred from state offices. Separate laws were maintained for Chinese and for the Mongols. Kublai Khan also reorganized the government, establishing three separate branches to deal with civilian (nonmilitary) affairs, to supervise the military and to keep an eye on major official.

A new capital city was constructed at present day Peking, China, in 1267.

Kublai was a great supporter of trade, science and the arts. He introduced the use of paper money. Kublai also established a system of sea transport and developed inland river and canal routes to move grain from the fertile rice-growing Yangtze River basin to the rest of his empire.

Contact with the West

Under Kublai, the opening of direct contact between China and the West was made possible by Mongol control of central Asian trade routes and aided by the presence of efficient postal services. In the early 13th century, large numbers of Europeans and central Asians made their way to China.

After a glorious reign of thirty-four years, Kublai Khan died in Ta-tu in February, 1294. He is regarded as one of the greatest rulers in history.

Genghis Khan

Kublai Khan

Remarkable people of the Middle Ages

Marco Polo

Marco Polo is well-known for his travels through Asia. He was one of the first Europeans to travel into Mongolia and China. Marco became famous for his book that told the story of his travels along the Silk Road to China.

Marco Polo was born in Venice, Italy around 1254. In 1271, when he was 17 years old, he travelled to Asia with his father and uncle. On this journey, he became a favourite of Kublai Khan, the Mongol Emperor.

In 1298, there was a conflict between Venice and Genoa. Polo was captured by the Genoese and imprisoned by them. While in jail, Marco dictated the story of his travels to a writer who published the book, 'The Travels of Marco Polo'. The book led to the explorations of Columbus and many others who were searching for a quicker way to sail to China and India.

William the Conqueror

William I, also known as William the Conqueror was the King of England. He was the son of the Duke of Normandy. In 1035 the Duke

set out upon a pilgrimage to the Holy Land in which he died. Before leaving for the pilgrimage, he presented William, who was then seven years old, to the nobles. Duke Robert made it clear to them that he expected complete allegiance to this young boy. He also placed William under the care of three guardians. But in due course of time, all these three men were murdered. It is noteworthy that in spite of this and of attempts to kidnap William, the child, after a period of turmoil, became the ruler of Normandy in his father's place.

William the Conqueror was important because he had established a new order in England. He ended the conflict between the Danes and the Saxons by establishing himself as the King.

Joan of Arc

Joan of Arc, (1412 - 1431) (Jeanne d'Arc in French), is a national heroine of France and a saint of the Catholic Church. During the Hundred Years War she led the French against the English and was ultimately captured and executed.

Joan was a peasant girl born in eastern France who claimed to have Divine guidance. She was captured by the Burgundians, sold to the English, tried by an ecclesiastical court, and burned at the stake when she was nineteen years old on the pretext of witchcraft. Twenty-five years after the execution, Pope Callixtus III examined the trial, pronounced her innocent and declared her a martyr. She was beatified in 1909 and canonized in 1920.

Thomas Beckett

Thomas Becket was the son of an English merchant who was born in 1118 in Normandy. His family was well-off, his father being the former Sheriff of London. Becket was sent to Paris for his education and from there to England where he joined the household of Theobold, the then Archbishop of Canterbury.

Becket's true success came in 1154, when Theobold introduced him to the newly crowned King, Henry II. The two liked each other immediately formed a strong bond. Henry made Becket his Chancellor. When Archbishop Theobold died in 1161, King Henry suggested the name of his loyal advisor Beckett for the highest ecclesiastical post in the land. The Pope agreed. The next day Beckett was ordained a Bishop and that afternoon, June 2, 1162, made Archbishop of Canterbury!

But King Henry's belief that Becket would support him in his misdeeds was not fulfilled.

And so, on December 29, the Archbishop Becket was brutally murdered by the King's men on the altar of the Canterbury cathedral, when a service was going on.

Test Your MEMORY

1. Which period in history is termed as the 'Middle Ages'?

2. What is Hagia Sophia. Write a short note on it.

3. Write briefly on Charlemagne, the memorable ruler.

4. Write few lines on the Mayan calendar.

5. Who discovered the ancient city of Macchu Picchu?

6. What does 'Yasodharapura' mean in Sanskrit?

7. Who were the Vikings? Write briefly about their social life.

8. What was Feudalism? Where did it flourish?

9. Write briefly about on one of the castles—Windsor or Edinburgh.

10. What were the Miracle and Morality plays?

11. What was Black Death? How did it affect the medieval world?

12. Discuss the effects of Crusades.

Index

A

Angkor Civilization 17
Angkor Vat 18

B

barons 21
Black Death 4, 25

C

Charlemagne 8, 9
Constantinople 5, 6, 7
Crusades 3, 26

D

Dark Ages 3, 9

E

Emperor Justinian 7

F

futhark 19

G

Gabriel 10, 11
Genghis Khan 27, 28
Gothic architecture 23

H

Haab 13
Hagia Sophia 7
Huitzilopochtli 14
Hundred Years War 4, 29

I

Islam 10, 11, 26

J

Jerusalem 3, 26

K

Kublai Khan 27, 28, 29

M

Machu Picchu 15, 16
Mecca 10, 11
Medina 11
Merovingian 8
Mesoamerica 12, 13, 14

P

Prophet 10, 11

Q

Quechua 15

R

renaissance 3, 4, 21, 23
runes 19

S

Saladin 26
Sapa Inca 15
Silk Road 4, 29
slavery 14, 19

T

The Travels of Marco Polo 29

Y

Yasodharapura 17